No Better Time Than This

by Robert Hale

Published by
YABISA GASHOUSE
C/ R. Curtoys Gotarredona, 1, Esc. 2, 2B
07840 Santa Eulària des Riu
Spain

ISBN-13: 978-84-949638-1-0

Read Robert's poetry at:
www.roberthale.info/poetry.html
www.nobettertimethanthis.tumblr.com

The moonbeam splinters night's skirt with light
Drink wine, there is no better time than this

Attributed to Ghiyāth ad-Dīn Abu'l-Fatḥ ʿOmar ibn Ibrāhīm
Khayyām Neīshāhpūrī
(Omar Khayyam, 1048-1131)
Persian scholar, polymath, philosopher, and poet.

Foreword

This is my first collection of verse. While from first to last these poems were written over quite a long period of time (the first is from 1994), most of them were written during the last three years. The main exceptions to this are the several three or four line poems, which I have inserted here and there among the longer poems. These very short poems are not listed in the table of contents. Many of my poems are inspired by my walks around the coastline of my home island of Ibiza, and by the moods conjured up by the landscape, seasons, and weather conditions. There is wonder at the marvels of nature around us, and anger at their desecration at the hands of human beings. There is also some social commentary, a small dose of whimsy, and of course love, the greatest motivator of all. I hope you enjoy reading these poems.

Santa Eulària des Riu, Eivissa[1], 21/12/17.

---

1   Eivissa is the local name for Ibiza, where a dialect of Catalan is spoken. When writing about my home island, I have used local names rather than their Castilian Spanish or English equivalents.

Contents

1. Sunrise over Sarajevo — 1
2. The World Through the Window — 3
3. A Scent of Long Ago — 4
4. Ways to the Sea — 5
5. To Watch from the Mala Costa — 7
6. Indifference — 8
7. In Invisibility — 10
8. The Back of the Bay — 13
9. A Hundred and One — 14
10. Little Bird — 17
11. Song to the Archetypal Forest — 19
12. Fingers of Love — 21
13. Remembrances (Men of Santa Agnès) — 23
14. The Watch — 25
15. The Gift — 28
16. Ordinary — 29
17. Extraordinary — 31
18. Kenyir - Just an Everyday Tragedy — 35
19. A Walk in Black and White — 38
20. Connection (I and I) — 39
21. It Is Different at Night — 41
22. A Well Kept Garden — 42
23. Sorry, Do I Know You? — 44
24. Line in Two Blues — 47
25. Round the Ferry Corner — 48
26. Always Now the Blackbird Calls — 49
27. Magon's Rock — 51
28. Boy on the Bank — 53
29. Crossroads — 55

30. Morning's Coast   56

31. The End of the Road   59

32. Nature's Healing Stuff   61

33. F-Art   62

34. Miseryguts   65

35. H2O   67

36. Death of a Perfect Poem   70

37. Aliens   72

38. Identity   73

39. Sawubona   75

40. Siesta Beach, 8th August, 7 a.m.   77

41. My Servants Called Me Mother   79

42. As Near as We Will Ever Be Again   81

43. Black Sun   83

44. Ignorant   84

45. In the Name of God   86

46. The Gardener of Kabul   91

47. Why I Do Not Lie for You   93

48. Out of Sight   95

49. No Signposts Now   96

50. Four Love Poems   99

To those who are precious to me.
To the wonder that is the world.
To the poets who have enthused me.
To the marvellous gift of mind that allows
us to appreciate precious things.

Lovely the Butterfly Flits

Lovely the butterfly flits
Dipping low, blown high
No hand shall contain her
For she would surely die

Santa Eulària, Eivissa, September 2002

If you perceive a disconnect in time and context between this first poem and all the rest, I ask forgiveness. It is here because, as it is one of the first poems I ever wrote, I have an affection for it. It is from way back when a brutal war raged in Bosnia-Herzegovina, and horrific atrocities were perpetrated. I had visited Sarajevo a few years beforehand, and being drawn to that beautiful city, was much saddened by what was taking place there. There is a mistake in the poem. The river running through Sarajevo is in fact the Miljacka, a tributary of the Bosna, but I have retained the original mistake as I like the sound of it. The poem is still contemporary as I write: for Sarajevo in 1994 you might just as well substitute Aleppo in 2017, it would not be much different...

Sunrise Over Sarajevo

One day the sun will rise
Over crumbling homes and broken towers
      and the dust of fallen stone,
Over the smoke on killing streets on the road
      to the stadium burial ground,
Over empty alleyways and squares
Where linger the clinks of long-absent hammers
      hammers
And the voices of long-departed crowds,
Over the college steps which knew the
      gatherings of youth
And the building of ideals and plans,
Over ghosts of Moslem, Christian and Jewish
      saints,
Over the deep red of the sullen Bosna river.

The sun will rise
Over the sky-turned faces of sense-blunted,
      blinking people,

Over quiet tears of deep soul-longing
For impossible half-forgotten dreams,
Over chilled, sickened, alienated human souls
And over the hardness of hearts
Tempered against any last nagging hope of
      deliverance;
Over the dead still of pregnant pre-dawn hours
When the mist comes up from the Bosna, the
      sun will rise
And rise again tomorrow
Over Sarajevo.

Treviso, Italy, February 1994

There is a popular bar in the alleyway beneath our balcony, with lively tables on the pavement outside, and beside them a public bench where sometimes in summer children gather to practise their Flamenco...

The World Through the Window

The curtains weave to a gentle push-pull
That through the open door brings in the night
Short-tempered waves crash and slide back
Thunder booms far out at sea
A soft, haunting symphony floats
From restless balcony chimes
Bar tables are moved, a rude chain
Is pulled around chair legs
A dog barks and is answered
A small neurotic motorbike
Whines frantic up the street
Laughing and joshing from the bench below
The Andalusian girls go clap, clap-clap
And cry out another anguished lament
As she and I lie wrapped
In our timeless world within

Santa Eulària, Eivissa, August 2011

Whenever I go to see my parents in Four Marks, Hampshire, I go for an evening walk up the lane behind the steam railway line near their home. Despite the recent industrial property development, the upper end of the lane, near Medstead station, is on the edge of the countryside and still quiet. The chestnut tree there is a friend of mine. The place has a magical feeling at night. One warm September night...

A Scent of Long Ago

A gibbous moon on the wane
Ursus Major lying low
A lone cricket gently calls
A heady scent of earth and leaf
And carried on the air
On tracks not bound by place
A scent of long ago

Four Marks, England, September 2014

I like to walk along cliffs and shorelines of Ibiza's rugged north coast. I composed this song while walking. I think it sounds good to the tune of Bob Dylan's *Absolutely Sweet Marie...*

Ways to the Sea

All paths lead to the sea but they ain't all easy
You might find an easy road but it won't be
      free
So I walk and I climb and I scrape till I get
      weary
Just to find what is waiting there for me
But what other way is there for it to be?

And you may find a hole which you can sleep
      in
And you may find a hole where the ground is
      hard
And you'll find to eat but the fruit ain't always
      juicy
And you may find to drink where the water's
      old
But what other way is there for it to be?

All our dead ends are just our limitations
No wings to fly way down this wild gulley
Where I'm sitting here to voice my
      incantations
Cicadas scream hypnotic from tree to tree
And what other way is there for it to be?

Cala d'Albarca, Eivissa, July 2015

Soulless Plain

Moon lifting large through flat mist -
On a brown soulless plain
The mad hare runs

Sacile, Italy, December 2009

The Serra de la Mala Costa is a range of hills in the north-east of Ibiza, from whose eastern slopes one can watch the sun rising from beyond the sea. If you are up there at dawn, you will likely be the only one around; a bit of a different feel from the Café del Mar in Sant Antoni de Portmany, where people flock to watch the sun set...

To Watch from the Mala Costa

To watch from the Mala Costa
At the birth time of the day,
The magic silent twilight burst;
The sun looks out to the western lay.
There, crowds will gather all in thirst,
To catch its glorious dying ray,
But I look East remembr'ing first
Another, solitary, silent way.

Sant Vicent, Eivissa, 2015

One of my entrenched behaviours is never to go walking with a group of people. There is so much beauty in the world around us which we miss or ignore in our urge to engage in a constant stream of communication. Sometimes silence is golden, but often we do not recognise those moments...

Indifference

A small motorbike screams to a climax,
Along the road to the river mouth.
At the bar drinkers converse in loud shouts
Across the two long yards from table to table.
Along the promenade people jabber as they
      walk,
About small injustices suffered and what
Somebody put on Facebook.
The night need not hide its jewels behind any
      cloud
But need not display them either.
And the sea retreats with equal disinterest
To everyone else's.
To the three casual witnesses to the scene,
The night, the moon and the lilting sea,
We are but a troop of fidgety, screeching
      baboons.

But for myself, is it too much to ask
For a little silence?

Creatures of vision,
What a splendid glittering shaft
Our satellite beams towards us
Across the gently rocking sea!

More precious than any jewel in any crown:
There are creatures that perish to claim it,
As, just hatched,
It pulls them to the water's edge.
Those beaches are far away from here.
As I walk now along this promenade,
The jabbering people
Give it neither glance nor thought.

And the night fades like a mist
Into a void of wasted time.

Creatures of sound,
What peace to hear the continual blow
And draw of an endless breath
Reach to us
From the world's ancient edge!
More meaningful than any book in any crypt:
There are those for whom it is the first
Breath and the last,
The constant driver of their lives.
Those beings are not here, not now.
As I walk here on these red slabs,
The jabberers jabber on
Staring all straight ahead.

As a wave retreats with a hiss
Into an ocean of indifference.

Santa Eulària, Eivissa, 2016

Some people always like to be the centre of attention and others shun attention like a nasty disease. But I am attracted to the idea that life is best approached strategically. If it were, we would not exhibit ourselves or hide away simply by force of habit, nor allow ourselves to be trapped by circumstance, but we would choose to be fluid, available to others, or otherwise, according to the moment, our needs, and those of others...

In Invisibility

Treading lightly
The line less trod,
The shadowed side,
Through mist,
As on a hollow way,
Well cocooned
By wraithlike curling boughs,
That no-one sees,
And neither,
They see me.

If anything
Just a suggestion,
A fleeting shadow,
Faintly flickering,
Melding with the mist,
Then gone,
And quickly disregarded,
As though never there.

Free to choose
If and when and why

To emerge,
To stand out
In the middle of the street,
In the sunlight,
Dressed perhaps
In a silver sequined coat;
To dance a jig
And sing a crazy song.
Out of tune.
Just so.
For a reason.
Then disappear at will.

Conegliano Veneto, Italy, February 2016

The Mountains Waltz

Melancholy plain, dim and grey
In fading light, while to the north
Mountains waltz in wedding cake white

Sacile, Italy, December 2009

A walk on a bright, windy day to one of my favourite places...

The Back of the Bay

I woke up at the dawn of the day
And I wandered up a pine-wooded way,
Then took myself down to the back of the bay,
Where the crags are sharp and the sun does
        play,
In glitter bright on the sea and the spray,
That roll and toss in the mouth of the bay.

And the wind is up and the waves are large,
Their blue so dark as in fury they charge,
And the gulls in the sky chatter and dive,
And I feel so fine and I feel so alive,
As along the cliff I make my way,
With the waves and wind at the back of the
        bay.

They ask me if I believe God exists.
Well, I say I'll allow that He is all this.
I don't try to know and I don't make a fuss,
As the waves do crash and the gulls do cuss.
'Cause the sight of this I think is enough.
And I'll come again along this way,
That takes me down to the back of the bay.

Cala d'Albarca, Eivissa, June 2016

My generation was not a materialistic one or an establishment one. We eschewed conspicuous consumption, designer brands, fashion, trendy places, big weddings (and even matrimony itself), proper jobs. We studied subjects we were interested in, which were usually those guaranteed not to make us much money, rather than those leading to normal professions or business success. We didn't want to become bankers, accountants, salesmen, even doctors or lawyers. We wanted to become environmentalists, oceanographers, anthropologists, beach bums, travellers and adventurers. Oh, and computer geeks, that hasn't changed. We wished to live simply according to our ideals, unburdened by established customs and money. But attitudes go round in wide circles, to an extent, and in these past couple of decades we are back with those of the 50s...

A Hundred and One

A hundred and one years, a hundred and one
We're all going to live to a hundred and one
And while we live to the age of a ton
We're gonna love and we're gonna have fun
We're gonna stay young and we'll dance in
      the sun
And we'll never have worries till our time is
      done

A thousand and two, now, a thousand and two
That's what we earn, a thousand and two
We pay the rent and the bills that are due
And we take a loan like the other people do
'Cause the SUV's old and we want one that's
      new
And we can't afford one on a thousand and
      two

A million and three blocks, a million and three
We're gonna build up a million and three
We'll cover the fields and cut down the trees
'Cause we're wasting the space with the birds
     and the bees
And now its worth money, it's a no brainer,
     please
So let's build up those blocks, a million and
     three

A billion and four bucks, a billion and four
I wanna make a billion and four
'Cause a million ain't nothing, it won't buy
     you a door
If you don't watch your back, I'll take you for
     more
I'll buy cheap and sell dear, on the edge of the
     law
For a billion and four bucks, a billion and four

Ten billion and five, though, ten billion and
     five
What do I want with a ten billion and five?
It's progress they say, it keeps men alive
But I no longer know for what do I strive
I fear for a loss, I can't well define
For now I am old at just sixty and five

A hundred and one years, a hundred and one
I ain't gonna live to a hundred and one
Where did my young hopes go, how were they
     undone?

Like a fool in my life I've done nothing but
    run
After things that now feel like the barrel of a
    gun
Many are the things I wish I had done
But complained of the rain and avoided the
    sun
And nothing but worry till my time is done
But I don't wanna die, I did wanna have fun
I wish I could live to a hundred and one

Santa Eulària, Eivissa, June 2016

There comes a time when we have to break out. In the young, it is a tender thing to see. Maybe we all need to keep doing it forever, or at least, till the end...

Little Bird

Little bird, perched quiet on a rock -
Wise one, it's the highest of the crop.
Watching now, your shiny black dot
Sees birth and life and death and rot.
Then you look to the line where the sight goes
      not,
And beyond to a world where your flight
      won't stop.

Below you the water's lapping in rhyme,
To the endless rhythm of the waves of time,
Sun warm on your back, breeze soft with
      brine,
And off the earth the scent of pine.
If this were your verse this would be your
      line:
"Open my wings for the time is mine!"

Little one, centre stage -
No thoughts you I'd wish in your timeless age,
But you'll fly best when the East winds rage.
Feel them ruffling your feathery maze.
Look up, fly high from those words on your
      page,
Fly fast, fly straight... through the roof of your
      cage.

Magic gathers on your high rock,
Where sight goes not but your flight won't
    stop,
Where the endless rhythm of the waves of
    time
Opens your wings when "the time is mine",
As the East wind breaks your timeless age
Fly fast and straight through the roof of the
    cage.

Sant Mateu, Eivissa, July 2016

Fire is an ancient and physiological part of the forest ecosystem. This poem is about the "disastrous" fire which struck the north-east of Ibiza in 2011...

Song to the Archetypal Forest

Today the spirit moves from the south;
the air is thick as I set out.
A hot wind fans this rugged land,
harsh and sweet as the desert sands.

I walk on ways where five years since,
high flames raged and the smoke was dense.
The pine trees burned, the birds flew fast;
all fled or died as the fire storm passed.

And when the flames were finally quenched
you saw a land where life was wrenched,
a smouldering waste, a landscape scarred,
stone walls scorched and tree stumps charred.

Yet even as people cried and railed
at the turns of fate, at certainties failed,
just as a fever will cleanse the flesh,
there's a force at work in the land afresh.

As I look on, five years hence,
on these ancient ways where pines were
        dense,
it's a strange, hard, beautiful, different world;
a new order begins to unfold.

Vital, clambering, fresh and strong:
a new world of colour and song.
I gaze on the hills in wonder and awe;
tenacity springs from every pore.

The archetypal forest's plan
is death and rebirth and to Hell with man's
other designs, his need to control,
ignoring the greater laws of old.

Large pines are gone, juniper too,
the land is rough, the trees are few.
The ones that stand are but hip height,
but all between, a glorious sight.

Now rosemary, lavender and rockrose reign,
butcher's broom and yellow fleabane,
wild thyme, heather, spiked ivy vine;
each singing a verse to the spirit's rhyme.

Sant Vicent, Eivissa, October 2016

The story of love is as old as humankind...

Fingers of Love

How long has passed
Since, as petals furled,
She curled
Her fingers round my heart?
How she held my gaze
And words, like floating leaves
She breathed
Strangely through the haze.
Thirty years ago, my dove,
I almost think
You might perhaps have been my love.
And I, for my part
Replied, but you
Perhaps, could break my heart
How long has passed?
Yet still,
As leaves of gold enfold
Those fingers hold me fast.

Santa Eulària, Eivissa, November 2016

I Am Willow

Silvery leaves, breeze-blown -
I freshen the valley where I stand
Beside the tumbling summer stream

Tramonti di Sopra, Italy, June 2010

It is a good thing sometimes, especially when in close contact with nature, to dispense with the safety net of thought and rationality, and just to feel...

Remembrances (Men of Santa Agnès)

Sometimes, travelling slow,
When the rain falls softly through the leaves,
Or the clouds hang grey in dawn's pale glow,
Or when night is thick and the darkness
     breathes,
Or the morning mist on the plain hangs low,
Or when gulls circle high as a black sea
     heaves,
And the pines on the cliff stand grey in a row,
Sometimes, then, quick on the breeze,
Come whispered voices from long ago.

November, mellow and still,
Waves rolling pebbles down on the shore,
Smoke rising up, over the hill,
The mood hypnotic, the feeling raw.
The air is pregnant, a vacuum to fill;
My senses attune to the land and its lore.
Then I can see and then I can feel
Memories coming from mankind's store,
For a second, then gone again, leaving a chill.

Sometimes, travelling blind,
The stuff of the world will quiver and shift,
For a second, a minute, a trick of the mind,

The wind will drop and a veil will lift.
There... Hear their voices, quick on the wind.
The men, they are coming, bound for the cliff,
Their idiom strange, they sing as they climb,
"We go to the boats, we go to fish,
We'll come back this way, if Our Lady is
      kind".

Santa Agnès, Eivissa, November 2016

On the rocky north coast of Ibiza there is a little known cave in a cliff face, of difficult access, where the men from the local village went to hide from the Guardia Civil during the Spanish Civil War of 1936-39. Sitting on a ledge outside this cave on a cloudy autumn day, overlooking a restless sea, I imagined what the thoughts of a man on guard duty might have been...

The Watch

How many hours have my eyes gazed upon
Those towers that jut from the oily sea?
I see them even in the night,
Immobile, jagged, tall and free.
Yet what will they, then, tell of me?
I know each crag, every angle of their lean,
The depth of shadow of each hollow and fold.
Waiting, watching, hour and day,
I know every tone of grey and gold.
I'll know this, too, when all is done and told.

So long have my senses pricked and thrilled
To the tireless call of the restless waves
Which thrash in the fibres of my flesh,
Nervous, brooding, wild and brave.
What can they know, of these men in this
      cave?
I know the moods, the lines of flow,
The deep dark trough, the frothing crest.
Waiting, listening, through to morn,
I know the cold and the fear no less.
I'll know it, too, when all is laid to rest.

How long have you shrilled and slapped my
    skin,
You headstrong wind that curls on the brine?
On these autumn days, that turn to chill,
You impetuous, maddening, lover of mine,
Do you carry my scent with thine?
I've known your summer whispered charms,
Your winter raging shrieks and yells.
Waiting, feeling, with every cell,
I know every tale my lover tells.
I'll know it still, at the final bell.

So long we've conversed, in chatter and song,
You gulls that plane and dive and sing.
We know each other so well, so long,
White darts, you masters of the wing.
Do you know, do you see what fate will bring?
I know your voice, the turn of your flight,
Your clucks and cries, the marks on your bill.
Waiting, watching, through to dusk,
I see in your eyes your thoughts, your will.
I'll know it, too, when blood will spill.

Would that I know my foe so well,
For finding me, he'll shoot me dead.
We were kids together, friends at school,
But now he would shoot me through the head.
And the story never will be read,
And all this, all this that I know,
Those towers, the sea, the wind, the gulls,
He'll have known them, too, our time, our
    place,

The soil, the sea, the sky and all.
He'll know my world, when he too shall fall.

Sant Mateu, Eivissa, November 2016

I was just standing on the beach after an evening swim, looking out on the bay, when...

The Gift

A little girl with hair so fair
Plucked a rainbow from the air,
A thing of beauty from the sand,
And put them gently in my hand.
Here lay a shell so small and white
The giver gone, flown, like a kite.
How strange that such a simple gift
Shall cause the tilt of the world to shift.

Santa Eulària, Eivissa, November 2016

In a pizzeria in a small town in northern Italy, that I have been familiar with over many years...

Ordinary

A sad pizza is put on the table
in a sad restaurant
where the people sit
where they always do
doing the same things
as they have always done.
Getting through life.
Staring at their phones.
Complaining,
about politics, the weather,
somebody else's doings.
Planning an outing
to the shopping mall
on a Sunday morning.
Some of them are kind
to each other because
things work nicely that way.
Some of them will take you
quickly for a profit
because they can.
Sitting at tables
in a sad restaurant
eating sad pizzas
getting through life,
growing old.
I have curved around the universe and back
      at the speed of light.

This is what I find.
A pizza is put on the table.
The waitress smiles a sad smile.
Does she know
this is as good as it gets?
Being ordinary
and not ever doing
an extraordinary thing.
Or thinking
an extraordinary thought.
Not many things will be extraordinary.
And not many poems either,
or even good.
I write one like that,
finish my sad pizza,
pay my sad money,
step into the rain
of an ordinary night.
Except, I realise too late
(having wasted precious time),
it isn't
so ordinary
at all.

Conegliano Veneto, Italy, November 2016

The moment when you realise every moment counts....

Extraordinary

Then you remember
a little girl
who gave you a shell
on a beach
just because you were there
and changed the world
for the better
but didn't know it.
What will become of her?
Will she ever sit
at a sad table
watching the people
do what they do,
what they have always done?
Will she ever put a sad pizza
on the table
with a sad smile
not knowing how once
she gave a bad poet
a lesson in life.
Out in the rain
you breathe,
There is an air
clear on your face,
cool on your eyes,
crystal in your mind.
Each new moment

of each new day
in each new world
each time you know
all you knew
does not have to be true,
you can decide
(and not by default)
to run the tide
with full heart,
sharp mind,
steady hands,
to make it through
or to fall
without complaint
and all the while
making it the greatest
thing you do.
I have curved around the universe and back
        at the speed of light.
This is what I find.
An extraordinary time.
A lesson sublime.
A poem that doesn't rhyme.
(Except, perhaps,
when it does).
To walk out in the night and,
looking up,
feel the rain on your skin
as you understand
all that is done,
all that is said
has made the world new,

a thing
nobody will ever undo.
A lesson learned
(again, for we who are dumb)
at a sad restaurant
on an ordinary night
in the rain.
When then,
you realise in time
(though none too soon),
it wasn't.
So.
Ordinary.
At all.

Conegliano Veneto, Italy, November 2016

34

The World Cries

The world sheds for her tears of sadness,
tears of joy; wide-eyed in wonder
she knows not why.

Santa Eulària, Eivissa, July 2010

In April 2016 Clouds Woman and I went back to her beloved Malaysia (my third time), and while we were there we stayed for a few days in a chalet on the shore of the vast, staggeringly beautiful, and still relatively unspoiled Lake Kenyir. On the other side of a bay near our quiet resort an eyesore of human activity was taking place, involving heavy earth-moving equipment. I asked a nature guide what it was all about, and what I was told became the basis of this sad and angry poem...

Kenyir - Just an Everyday Tragedy

A long red gash is open on her body;
I wince because her pain is also mine.

The people who cut her are back
Cauterizing her wound with black
Tarmac in a rectangle: a park
For a thousand cars and more
Of city folk who'll come (they hope)
To power fifteen miles up the shore
From a smart pleasure port
On a fast motor launch
To their four-star hotels,
And enjoy the delights
Of a shopping mall
On a pretty island
In the lake.
Duty-free.

For which the forest there is torn,
And nothing left to mourn its passing.

Only the Earth will cry, and I will feel her
        pain,
Because what is hers is also mine.

Emerald fingers of her generous lymph
Snake vastly, stellate, up the valleys
Since they were drowned,
And all life in them, too,
To quench the thirst
Not for water
But power.

Notwithstanding, she is yet beautiful.
Her gathered lymph yields new life,
New places to live, until
The foulness and clatter
Of trippers' boats
Kills it again
For a shopping experience.

I would wish to relinquish my belonging to
        my race
And live with those long-tailed macaques
I see in the trees.
That is, if they, those others,
Would not come and drown my home,
Dirty the waters they had made,
And build a mall on my last retreat.

And few but the Earth would mourn,
Who too, would feel my pain,
Because my loss were also hers.

Considering this, I just better stick around,
Doing tiny deeds of defiance,
(Subversively from within),
Like this one,
To tell you about
Just an everyday tragedy.

Santa Eulària, Eivissa, December 2016

Walking along the Santa Eulalia seafront to the "river" mouth then up the creek to the old bridge on a winter's evening. Not many people around. Here are a few snapshots...

A Walk in Black and White

Along a white path upon a black night
Thoughts of the day all taking flight
A white thin moon hangs in a black sky
A star so bright travelling with it so high
A white heron hunts by the black of the sea
In its beak something silvery flaps to be free
A white bridge stands low, before a black hill
So many years so silent, so still
A white duck floats upon a black pool
Like a white pearl set against a black jewel

Santa Eulària, Eivissa, December 2016

For Bob, myself, and all loving fathers...

Connection (I and I)

I dreamed I was two
stuck as with glue
or overlapping like ripples
converging on a pond.
I turned and asked what
is this strange split.
He said I am you, you are me,
we are one.
And it was my son.

Santa Eulària, Eivissa, December 2016

She Is the Moon

Riding bright
Over the domes and towers of her youth
She sails like the moon

Santa Eulària, Eivissa, July 2010

I love the dark of the night, especially in the countryside. It reveals a whole new world where things appear to us and affect us differently than they do during the daytime. Its unfamiliarity causes anxiety in some people, but others are thrilled and enthused by its mystery and lack of fixity or certainty...

It Is Different at Night

It is different at night:
Shadows obey the words of the wind,
Scents from the earth wake sleeping things,
Unearthly shapes on silent wings;
Nothing is quite as tame as it seems
Under daytime's lantern bright.

You creatures of blinding sight
To objects rude and sharp are bound,
Certainties fixed, judgements sound,
Your gritty wheels of reason pound
All mystery from the solid ground,
Till the waning of the light.

But we hunters of the night,
By fate and chances we were born,
To fly on the winds of gathering storms,
To stalk our mystery prey till dawn
Of a pearly icicle morn,
When the sky is silent, heavy, and white.

Yes, it is different in the night.

Santa Eulària, Eivissa, December 2016

The cemetery adjoining the old Church on the hill above Santa Eulalia is a very peaceful place to stop, for a few minutes or an eternity...

A Well Kept Garden

Yes, they may have had their ways,
Done, at times, as they would not
Be done by, committed trespasses
Small or large, born malice,
Spoken words unjust, which
From time to time, perhaps,
Went unconfessed on Sunday.
Yet the eyes of these folk are good
As they gaze from the sills
Of their cold polished slabs.

It is a well kept garden, this,
With its swept paths dividing
Neat flower beds and squares
Of trimmed and watered lawn.
A rake, a broom, a bin for cuttings
Tidily stored in a corner.
And orderly, terraced rows
Of fine multi-story accommodations
For the good folk of this town.

Adorned most with bright flowers -
Plastic (on discrete inspection),
But cheerful nevertheless.
Though some façades are faceless,

With no good eyes gazing out,
And slab-less too,
Just initials scrawled, and dates,
In crayon on concrete,
And a grubby plastic bloom
Lonely on the sill.

My footsteps sound on the path.
Children's shouts and shrieks
Filter through from the church front.
The quiet here is not soundless,
But of a deeper, more solid kind.
Sunlight glances down in beams
On these good, unseeing folk.
For rich and poor,
Cherished and forgotten,
It is a glad place to lie.

Santa Eulària, Eivissa, December 2016[2]

---

2   First published in *Poetry Quarterly*, Issue #31 (Fall 2017), Prolific Press, 2018.

Take-Away-Clouds-Woman isn't so young any more and she can't
remember everything. Don't be offended, please, if you stop her on
the street and she says...

Sorry, Do I Know You?

I'm very sorry but I haven't a clue
who you are.
That's the answer to,
Chloe! I haven't seen you for ages!
How are you?

Every day in town I do the round
and people stop me on the street,
to greet me like a long lost friend
and throw their arms around me.
Boy, I must have been popular once!

That was when we had the house
and the gallery.
Every Sunday I made a pot
of Indian curry
to feed a regiment or a school,
and served it by the pool.

People came and lay around,
some of them I knew,
artists, actors, singers, writers,
there were quite a few,
they all brought other people,
and some scroungers, too.

But I didn't mind, it was such fun,
the laughter, talk and banter,
and such an interesting crew.

Many just acquaintances,
not all good friends, I know,
"associates", Muhammad Ali called them
on the Parkinson Show.
Funny what you remember, though.

But so many interesting people,
what's happened to them all?
I think perhaps they've gone to ground,
cleared off out of town
or died of the drink, the rot, or age,
extinguished like the dinosaurs,
the times aren't with them now.

Maybe they are the ones,
(but I think probably not)
the ones who stop me in the street
(it happens quite a lot).
I used to bluff through it quite decently,
but now I find honesty
is the best policy,
and less tiring, certainly.
So now I just say (brazenly),
I'm very sorry, my memory's shot,
I haven't a clue, please tell me,
who are you?

Santa Eulària, Eivissa, December 2016

When the Moon Tilts

When the moon tilts water tips out
Clouds Woman says, and tomorrow
Rain's perfume floats on the morning

Santa Eulària, Eivissa, July 2010

Early on a fine winter's morning I walked out of Santa Eulalia, heading north-east along the coast path. At some point before I reached S'Argamassa, the sun rose...

Line in Two Blues

A blob of orange-gold slides molten

Over the line in two blues

Where sea meets sky

On a January morning

Of crystal brilliance.

Taking form, it climbs the lesser blue

Warming my seaward side

As I walk.

A white heron, disturbed,

Launches heavily from the shallows

Trailing stalky legs,

Veering east.

A cormorant, nervous,

Cranes its neck,

Dives from its rock

To boisterous white tops

Licked by gusts of chill

From round Cap LLibrell.

Santa Eulària, Eivissa, January 2017

A scent brings back fond, forgotten memories...

Round Ferry Corner

Round the ferry corner, the smell
Of drying seaweed slaps me alert.
Memories of bladderwrack carpets,
Slippery on a pebbly beach.
We squeezed the slimy vesicles
To make them pop.
Draped fronds on our heads
To make a horrid, viscid wig.
I remember a composite
Of many seaweed carpets
On many pebbly beaches
From sunshine times of yore.
I strive to hold the salt, musty, fishy scent
Through cigarette smoke and cheap perfume
Of people passing by.
In vain. But maybe I'll walk
This way again.

Santa Eulària, Eivissa, January 2017

Sometimes some cue or combination of cues in the environment - the colour of the sky, the stillness of the air, the time of year, the quality of the light, the call of a bird - conjure up feelings and images from years ago. As a child and teenager I was an avid fisherman and my favourite fishing places were the lesser rivers of Berkshire. In one way this poem is about that. But it is also about recognising the auspicious moment, and seizing the chance that comes our way...

Always Now the Blackbird Calls

Like as not you've but one chance
Before the moment passes,
The moment the blackbird calls.
On those strange winter evenings
Of cut-glass air and spectral light,
That darkens by the second.
When a cool yellow band stretches wide
Between blue-black banks of cloud
And black, flat, lonely land.
When the chill descends rapidly,
On a land wanting of small comfort,
From the weak, white sun,
Now fallen beyond the Earth's edge.
The world readies for a long night.
The wind will have dropped
Twenty minutes past.
The gurgling rush of the river
Is the only sound. Its inky swirls
Push the rushes roughly
In a bouncing, circular sway.

It is always now the blackbird calls;
Then flies in a low dip to the hawthorns,
Dark on the opposite bank.
It is always now the big chub bites,
And like as not you've but one chance.

Santa Eulària, Eivissa, February 2017[3] [4]

---

3   A chub is a European freshwater fish.
4   First published in *Poetry Quarterly*, Issue #31 (Fall 2017), Prolific Press, 2018.

Tagomago is a small island just off the north-east coast of Ibiza. It is said its name derives from that of one of the great Carthaginian general Hannibal's brothers, Magón. Under Islamic rule it was known as Taj Umayu. Around the time I walked by, despite the grey sky and the cool wind, the almonds were just coming into blossom...

Magon's Rock

Magon's rock lying sombre,
Flat between stone-grey sea
And darkly brooding sky,
Like a great black beast
Quiet, semi-submerged:
The dragon I fancy,
Resting perhaps,
On its timely flight
Marking coming spring.
For look there, friends!
Almond has blossomed.

Pou d'es Lleo, Eivissa, February 2017 [5]

---

5   In ancient China it was believed that spring was brought by the passing of a dragon.

Hot Rocks

Thyme-scented warmth off sun-baked stone,
Running-through-rocks-water lovely below,
Pyrites a glittery treasure trove.

Terre Rouge, Alès, France, September 2010

Bodies of water have held a sense of mystery and fascination for me ever since my childhood. Here's where it started, at the pond in Priory Park, Southend-on-Sea, where every day was a sunny summer's day...

Boy on the Bank

Boy on the bank, a picture
Of timeless intent, forever
Held by a mystery world
Whose surface is a dusty mirror
Reflecting placid summer trees,
While deep within move unknown things.

I cannot see, but know
A knob of bread
Is pressed about a pin,
Bent, on a string,
Dropped from the cane
In the boy's hand;
He, seated on the sand
On a sunny day
In shades of grey
On Ilford photographic paper.

Strange lives are lived down in the murk,
Removed from the airy upper world
Where sunlight warms a boy's hair,
A playful zephyr strokes his cheek,
Excited cries of children
Carry on the breeze, to reach
But not to keep

His attention.

His eyes are fixed on a Lego brick,
Floating white on black,
Over his suspended line,
And he suspended, too, in time.
Not stirring to the float's slow drift,
To bobble or gust or ripple,
Yet thrilling to any shiver or flick,
Hardly seen and lightning quick,
A signal from below.

But though, then, he did not know
Mystery was the bait,
And he was hooked, and fast,
Those many years ago.

And now he sits looking back through time
To the boy on the bank with his rod and line.

Santa Eulària, Eivissa, March 2017

From nearby Tanit's Cave in the hills above the tiny village of Sant Vicent, a small path leads down a wooded valley to a torrent bed, dry except after heavy rain. There it meets, and crosses, another path...

Crossroads

Standing at a crossing of paths;
paths of earth and rock that snake
through pine and thyme; and time.
A lattice of prints across the land.
This way to the hills.
That one to the bay.
This to the town,
and that to a thin blue line
a light year away.

See the pattern that marks our land!
The richly criss-cross weave,
the warp and weft, we left
in time and place; of men
and women's aims, and aimlessness.
From our beginning
to our today.
And tomorrow
whither goes the way?

Sant Vicent, Eivissa, March 2017

Walking the north-east coast of Ibiza from Cap de Can Negret to S'Escullet, 8th March 2017. Tanit, Phoenician and Carthaginian goddess of war, motherly love, and fertility, looks down on this coastline from her cave-shrine high in the hills above...

Morning's Coast

Dawn breaks on Morning's Coast
Orange-cream and pyric,
Of razor rocks, volcanic,
Like fair, terrible Tanit,
Who watches from her lair.

Sun up on Morning's Coast.
Silver glints off inky waves,
Like treasure lost in sunken caves
Of pirates brutal, rude and brave,
Whose breath still mists the air.

Wind falls on Morning's Coast
In bitter blasts or whispers mild,
Now playing coy, now yelling wild,
Now like the mother, now the child,
Now like a lover's touch so rare.

Sea up on Morning's Coast,
Brisk as joy, or white as death,
Breathing of the Levant breath,
Sculpting splendid ruggedness,
Of crumbling cliffs and boulders bare.

Land fall on Morning's Coast,

Men of Tiber and Phoenicia,
Weathered Argonauts tenacious,
Their gods both cruel and gracious,
Above them all, Tanit the fair.

Sant Vicent, Eivissa, March 2017

Friendship

Together, with talk of strife,
love and life,
this bitter sweet wine tastes good

Terre Rouge, Alès, France, September 2010

Sometimes one thinks, if it came to that, "How would I do it?" Personally, I've always dreamed of flying, but I've never liked spectators. Punta des Far, Formentera, in winter is a suitably dramatic yet secluded location to take flight for a few seconds, before the end...

The End of the Road

Found under a stone at Punta des Far,
        Formentera ...

How did I end up here?
It's been a long road, it's true,
with many bends and forks,
and many landscapes too.
But now, if I look back,
the way is straight and dead and flat
as far as I can see.

This is, I think, the end of the road,
at a lighthouse car park,
on a lonely, treeless headland.
The taxi is now just a receding dot,
like so many things.

I walk the few remaining steps,
and sit.
Before me the sky and sea
stretch as one to infinity,
as flat as the morning,
as grey as the hole in my chest.
They seem to reach for me.

The morning is better for it, I'd said,
the evening would be just too dread.

How can the air be so still?
Expectant, as a void to fill.
Something must happen soon.
Far below in slow motion
whiteness blooms on jagged stone.
Anyone falling from this height
would smash to gory bits
of flesh and bone.
Not a pretty sight.
But I've always dreamed of flight.
So even here, even now,
I am capable of humour.
But am I of desperation?
Or if not, abandon?

I move a little closer.
take out a pencil, a scrap of paper
to write down these my thoughts.
For what?
Is this, then, the end of the road?

Santa Eulària, Eivissa, March 2017[6]

---

6   First published in *Tears*, New York Literary Magazine, November 2017.

Springtime is pure joy wandering over the Ibiza hillsides, with the island still fresh from winter rainfall and the wild flowers running riot with explosive energy...

Nature's Healing Stuff

Yes, this truly is nature's healing stuff,
This symphony of colour and scent,
Live, alive, on the hills.
Soft unthinking joy is the healing way;
Doctor, you cannot separate it,
Bottled, to cure man's ills.
No remedy in your book compares one tenth
To the wild, glorious riot of life,
That here, mind and body fills.

Sant Vicent, Eivissa, March 2017

I have a line in cynicism and naturally this appears in some of my poems, this one for instance, about the enormous pretence endemic among both the artistic intelligentsia and the celebrity echelons of the arts and popular culture...

F-Art

I know what they want, by gad I do!
Over-shoulder shouting as they lead me
       away... ha!

Pieces of my brain roughly diced, laid
       interestingly in pairs.
A crimson smear artful across the plate, à la
       Masterchef.

I won't be like that other loser. No Man no!
"Makes food that people want to eat", they
       judged.

The fool! The madness!
Madness? I'll give you madness, Sir!

Let me take your gravy jug
and hurl it across your stark white wall.

Shit-brown splats trickle down fascinatingly,
making for fine dining indeed at the Tate.

Where sophisticated patrons know beautiful
       paintings
are not art but merely decoration.

I release a fart.
And not before time either.

Will encase it in perspex for visitors to sniff,
enthralled by the invisibility of this richly
          creative effort.

Label it "F-Art". Golly gee!
This boy's a genius, they will agree.

And a melodious one, yeah!
A rare expression of truth and life in this
          place.

But ignored. They shall not allow naive
          melody
to distract from their shiny new Zeitgeist.

In this day and age? Strewth!
Let us cut our hair differently and go forward.

Of course I know full well they are happy
who are not delighted by delightful things.

Perplexing that the teacher, though,
perhaps had something else in mind... what
          say?

I take a hike, going forward, shining my
          Zeitgeist.
Looking for laughs after this display, but thin
          on the ground.

Funny comedians stacked at the undertakers
    office.
Outside, a vicious flock of boars ploughs the
    earth for nastiness.

What a hoot! How you roar at all the right
    moments!
Another sonorous collection of gasses freed.

Needing some choice words to thrust me
    beyond range,
I put my ear to the flags in curiosity. What
    goes?

There! The poet cuts a clod of seven-coloured
    prose,
pegs bits out in twos like laundered socks on a
    line.

Hey Presto! You have F-Art. Truthfully,
    vitally,
its plastic, unappealing self.

Santa Eulària, Eivissa, April 2017

I suffered my teenage years sometimes quite acutely. Ever since then I have sought solitude, but never again felt lonely or unhappy about it. In fact, one of the times I am happiest is when wandering, with "only" the wind, the waters, the trees, the land, the sky, and all that immensity for company...

Miseryguts

Someone said I was boring, a lanky git,
Made me feel inadequate.
They called me Miseryguts, quiet and odd,
Made me feel misunderstood.
Someone called me unsociable, beyond a
    prayer,
... By then I didn't care.
Someone said he keeps to himself, way to be?
But by then I felt free.
Someone said and someone said, but I couldn't
    hear
With the whispering breeze and the singing
    sea.
I listened to those voices
And I felt joyous.

Santa Eulària, Eivissa, June 2017

Firmament Embrace

Amid night's vast expanse
A million-candled chandelier
Lights a lovers' embrace

Terre Rouge, Alès, France, September 2010

I have always loved bodies of water - streams, rivers, lakes, and sea - which I have walked by, swum in, fished in and sometimes drunk from since childhood. I have taken the example of water for this poem about how we know things, indeed, how we know our world...

H2O

They taught me,
In Science and in Chemistry,
How atoms combine two to one
(according to their valency)
Of hydrogen to oxygen.
And how, because of surface tension
From hydrogen bonds
A belly flop hurts like hell
And insects with hydrophobic legs
Can skate across the pond.
They taught me in Physics classes
Of water's different phases,
Boiling and freezing points,
Specific gravity and the like,
And how it makes a spectrum
By refracting the light.
And its properties as a solvent,
Important in Biology,
As a medium for reactions,
Essential for life.
They taught me its percentages:
60, by weight, of human body mass
And 70, by area,
Of the surface of the Earth.

That was in Geography
Where they taught things of other sorts:
How we build towns beside it,
Use it for trade and for transport,
And how it forms a natural border
For politics and nationhood.

These are some things about H2O
They taught me at school -
All very interesting and all very good.
Black and white, solid facts,
And I wrote them all down
On white in black.

But they didn't teach me magic
(In Physics, Maths or Chemistry,
Biology, Art, or Music,
History, Sport, Geography).
Like the magic in the pouring rain
Watched trickling down the window pain.
Or the taste of a cool glass drunk
On a hot and thirsty day.
Like the glitter in a dewdrop on a clover leaf.
Like the slap of storm drops on a tent's fabric
        roof.
The dank chill of air in the depths of a cave.
The fear of a fight against raging waves.
Steam rising from the valley after the rain.
The joy of a swim through the bouncing brine.
A cloudburst way out over a sea so grey.
Mist off the river at dawn in May.
An icy shower under a high waterfall.

The pounding power of the Devil's
      punchbowl.
The pebbles on the shore that rattle and ring.
The chattering song of a mountain stream.
The fury of the same in a snow water spate.
The smell of the churn through a weir gate.
The delight of a spot by the white willow tree.
The life of the river from spring to estuary.

These are some things about water
I found out along the way -
Colourful and undisciplined,
Gifts of joy and gifts of awe.
You can hear them in my voice
And see them in my eyes.
Facts made me a little clever,
But these things a little wise.

Santa Eulària, Eivissa, June 2017

Love is not all plain sailing. Sadly, sometimes discord appears as if from nowhere, even in what one might have thought were the perfect set of circumstances for harmony and romance. These things can turn on small matters: the wrong word said, a button pressed, a fatal misunderstanding...

Death of a Perfect Poem

The poem began with sublime perfection:
A geranium moon slipped slowly from a sea
As flat as the salt plains of Dasht-e Kavir,
And a dark purple sky so solid one might
Just reach up and break off a piece.
Shaking off the drips, it threw a shimmery
    band
Straight across the water like a hand
And clad us each with silver leaf.

We watched it rapt, you and I
Slide west across the perfect sky,
Stopped in time yet fast and high
Enough to follow with naked eye.

The poem turned and changed its form
When the moon soared high across the Isle,
With its black hump and its lizard's smile,
But the lizard's eyes were watching
That globe, and saw, a fiery bee.
Its mouth gaped and its tongue flicked,
But the moon flew fast and the lizard licked
Only the silver from the sea.

You said now look, there's a change,
Its just an ordinary moon again,
The spell was broke just when you spoke,
But you and I with the moon above
Drinking wine in the warmth of night,
Raised glasses to its onward flight,
In our eyes, ahead, a night of love.

The moon had passed the lizards tail,
Now white and small on a sea of black,
But the poem had fallen on its back,
Its thoughts conflicting one with t'other,
Its words confused, sore and sharp,
Its mood grew darker line by line,
It grasped for rhyme and gasped for time,
And there the poem just gave up.

Jarring words were said,
The magic veil was shed.
The moon grew small, and hid
Its face behind a wall of cloud,
Its pretty silver train
Now sadly thin, and sickly pale
Dissolving on the ripply waves
And that was how the poem expired
That night
It lived, it loved, it tried, but lost
Its light
And died.

Santa Eulària, Eivissa, June 2017

I am fascinated by what and how other creatures experience the world, how do they experience emotions, if at all, and whether they think, to what extent, and in what form. We can never know these things. If you could be an insect, a bird, or a fish, for one hour, how alien would you find it, and how faithfully could you describe the experience afterwards..?

Aliens

She comes to me a-zig a-zag -
Blue dragon whirring, inches from my face.
Many Eyes, what do you make of me?

A cobalt flash dazzles the valley dark:
An instant of beauty, ever to delight.
Fisher King, what are you delighted by?

We meet deep on a cool shingle run.
Close, you stare through my glass.
Golden Gills, how does the water feel?

At the boundary of our worlds
We meet, but cannot share.
We see, but neither as the other sees.

Santa Eulària, Eivissa, July 2017[7]

---

7   The first three lines were first published as a standalone poem in *Three Line Poetry Issue 44*, Prolific Press Inc., 2017.

How would you answer the question, "Who are you?" I am interested in our sense of personal identity. I also find it very interesting how our perceptions of other people's identities are distorted and limited by our tendency to pigeon-hole complex phenomena into facile categories, often depending on the context. It is curious to me, too, how people (even extroverts, no... particularly extroverts!) usually show extraordinarily little inclination to find out much of any substance about the people they meet...

Identity

I am my name
I am her current man
I am a member of the band

I am a friend of the groom
I always stand at the end of the room
I got rich in the housing boom

I am my own boss
I'm always cross
I am at a loss

I am the team leader
I am a maths teacher
I am a lay preacher

I am from a middle class family
I didn't go to a top university
Sorry to disappoint, obviously

I'm respected in the neighbourhood
I'm well connected, that's understood
I'm a member of the brotherhood

I don't know Professor Chi I fear
But I know many people here
Actually none, to be quite clear

I am just here to inspect the roses
I'm not interested in all these poses
Of you and all your cronies

When you asked me who
Which answer interested you?
Well, goodbye, and toodle-oo.

Santa Eulària, Eivissa, July 2017

Sawubona is a Zulu greeting which translates as "I see you." But really it means more than this. Somebody who says this to you is saying he or she recognises your personality, humanity and dignity...

Sawubona

Sawubona, I see you
I see your pain
I see it's not in vain
I see your deepest need
I see you are your affinities
I see you are an ocean wave
That withdraws but comes again
I see you are a mayfly
That lives and dies in a day
I see you are a salmon
That strives every inch of the way
I see your strength is reason
As well as your limitation
I see you are what you defend
Your work your love your patience
I see you are the world you see
I see you are your dignity
I see you are your freedom
I see you are your bonds
I see you are your fate
I see you are your path
I see you are your love

I see you are your heart
Sawubona, I see you

Santa Eulària, Eivissa, July 2017

A darkly cynical poem. One often hears it said or written about my home island that it is "paradise". This is pure humbug and hyperbole. In places it is extremely beautiful, in others it can inspire the kinds of sentiments expressed in this poem. I do not believe, as I have heard it said, that humankind is the ordained guardian of the planet. I think that in the greater scheme of things, when all is said and done, what we do here and what becomes of us may not be important even one iota. Yet here and now, and for the quality of life of my children and theirs, from my non-important, temporal, subjective perspective, I care; and as a principle of life I try to behave as if it were important...

Siesta Beach, 8th August, 7 a.m.

The world has had a sweaty, restless night.
A tangerine sun squints, befuddled, through
      the eastern haze.
A peevish sea jabs, in boredom, at brown
      weary rocks.
Leaden air paws, oppressive, regressive, at
      your prickly skin,
Makes you trip and swear. The world
Casts a cynic's eye, says there!

Not-so-old walls of cement and sea water
      submit
Passively to time and indifference.
Cracked, decaying, broken, dying, taking
Their pointless graffiti with them.
Palm fronds and cuttings from verdant
      gardens
Dumped here in blithe contempt.

They whine for respect but afford us none
And our dignity crumbles and falls
Like the broken, rotten walls.

A red, rough, stony path,
Scrubby verges of lank grass,
Plenty dog shit, much variety,
(Amongst cuttings from the topiary),
Fresh and soft; or rotting, old and dry,
In brown, black, green, dull grey, chalk white,
Competes for space with beer cans, plastic
        bags,
Crisp packets, water bottles, torn up rags,
Burger boxes, paper wrappings, ends of fags.
Then concrete platforms built for bathing in
        the sun,
Abandoned all to flows of grime and mulch
        and dung.

And the sad dusty path is dry as bone,
Except where a garden's dribbling hose
Makes muddy puddles here and there, and
        where
You slip and fall and swear. The world
Casts you a jaundiced glare, says there!
You want to know how and you want to ask
        why,
But the world squeals deafening, shrill and
        high,
Like a festering sow in a foul pigsty.

Santa Eulària, Eivissa, August 2017

This poem is about an ugly encounter experienced by a friend of mine...

My Servants Called Me Mother

You know

My servants called me Mother, she said
And her eyes were hard and her jaw was set

And I was good to you, she said
And her eyes narrowed, her nostrils flared

You are beneath me, she said
And her eyes bulged and her teeth were bared

You don't belong here Kaffir, she said
And her eyes were rage and her face was red

Goddam stupid Bongwe, she said
And her eyes burned in her hating head

You should be in the jungle, she said
And her words spat and her face was dread

You chilli bite, you stink, she said
And her words were growled and her face was
          lead

And you know

My servants called me Mother, she said,
And she closed her heart and she turned and
 fled

Santa Eulària, Eivissa, August 2017

Every day at dawn when I go down to swim, a middle-aged Oriental couple sit on the concrete ledge under the sea wall and gaze out to the rising sun. I wonder what they are thinking...

As Near as We Will Ever Be Again

Over where the sky is brightening they'll be
    eating Yeung Chow
But this is just about as far from home as we
    can go
Yet we are as near as we will ever be again
And summer after summer hurtle by us like a
    train
Sitting on the sea wall here at daybreak with
    my wife
Silent, impassive, thoughts of fate, thoughts of
    life
Looking to the rising sun, transported on its
    rays
Born home a precious moment by the power
    of our gaze

Santa Eulària, Eivissa, September 2017

Soft September

Soft September
Breathes gently
Her lover's breath on my back

Santa Eulària, Eivissa, September 2010

Not all poetry can by uplifting. This one is a nightmare...

Black Sun

I dreamt I fell asleep and dreamt I dreamt
That I awoke but all the world was changed
My room was wrong, its lines were bent
And water circled backwards down the drain
Outside the sun was as black as ink
In a sky so red that darkened as it climbed
Till at its height all was black as pitch
And nothing could be seen of sky or land
No lights, no moon, no stars, no shapes
Till through the afternoon a bleeding line of
    sky
Paled until to the leaden sea it dropped
And then I woke for a second time
And remembered what had passed the day
    before
And the sun in my heart turned black and cold
And the blood in my veins ran thick and slow
And I went to the window and saw that globe
Hanging black in a terrible blood-dark sky
And a sob from the heart of a world bereft
Came from my throat in an endless cry
And I asked myself, what is left
And I asked myself as I called your name
Can this be real? Can this be sane?
And I asked myself and I called my name
Is there any way back from this again?

Santa Eulària, Eivissa, September 2017

Yes, yes, I know there are unscrupulous people out there who get together to achieve world domination through unspeakable means. It's just that I think it is a much less all-consuming and a much more chaotic phenomenon than the conspiracy theorists would have it, and it certainly doesn't excite me as much as it does them. But of course, they are so much cleverer than people like me. We are all naive, gullible, ignorant, you see...

Ignorant

Come on, open your eyes he said
Wake up and use your brain
It's clear as day
Don't you see?
Its just a damned conspiracy
With multinational companies
To keep us all on our knees
And governments just tell us lies
They never went to the moon, you fool
They spent the money on bombs instead
Made enemies to make the money flow
And everyone should know
That nine eleven was a government plot
To control us all, and ignorance
Is by far the best
Weapon they've got

You know they're trying to poison us he said
Pointing to the sky
What? I said, and Where? and he said there
Those trails are not just jets
They want to make us ill and die

To keep their profits up
And how? I asked in dread
It's on the Internet he said
But you have to know which sites to read
The ones that tell the truth about
Their corruption and their greed
And who? I asked. Poor boy
They've got your brain he said
You'd better wake up or you
Will soon be lying sick or dead

Nine tenths of the world is ignorant he said
But I've studied medicine, he meant
He'd read some stuff on the Internet
I've done research. What in the lab
Or in the field? I asked
He looked at me aslant
You've gotta get aware!
On Google, it's all there!
He'd found out the cause of cancer
Which they hide from us because
Get this right in your head
Medicines are just to make us ill
They want to keep us ignorant, and how!
Its all big business, then he said
And boy! their profits are sure for now
And you, you're just a fat milk cow
I know, I read it on the web
Get it in your head
Or you'll soon be dead

Santa Eulària, Eivissa, October 2017

I was very moved by a BBC news report of 20th October 2017 about Raqqah stadium. The group called Islamic State made their last stand in Raqqah at the stadium on 17th October 2017. They had been using it as a prison and a place of "interrogation" and slaughter. I sat down and wrote this poem. It was raw, unpolished, and that is the way it has stayed...

In the Name of God

And now the time has come to fulfil my
    childhood dream
To walk up those steps at the end of this
    tunnel
And out into the light and onto the pitch and
    look up to the stands
And I will pretend now that there are crowds
    to cheer
Instead of sombre silence
And fresh green turf beneath my feet
Instead of blood-soaked dirt
And instead of praying to God for goals and
    victory
I will pray for a painless death and paradise
I have been moving up this passage for
    twenty-eight days
And each day I have prayed for this moment
Twenty-eight days scratched in lines on my
    wall
Did I say "my" wall? Mine at least
Since I was first put into that stinking hole
At the far end of this corridor
From where now I am led
And since I first heard the hideous screams

echoing along it
And the awful moaning that never stopped
I heard them still
Even with my hands clamped over my ears
As I lay curled in a shivering ball in the corner
Among the rat droppings and stench
Of urine, fear, blood and death
I prayed for this moment every time the men
          came
First they took me to the next room up
For the simple beatings
Day after day
And I prayed
Then they took me one room further along
To be strapped to an iron bed for two hundred
And twenty volts to be shot through my body
          like thunderbolts
A few seconds of Hell, and I mean Hell
Time and time and time again
And I prayed
Then one room further up this tunnel again
To be hung by chains from the roof by my
          wrists
And beaten with rods, my feet, my limbs,
My body, my genitals, and left, hanging
For hours on end and then
To be beaten again
And I could hardly pray
And when, in the last room
They stretched and bent my body
Beyond its limits and those of my sanity
With gym machinery that once my heroes
          used

Before it was changed to cause pain and
      mutilation
Diabolically, in the name of God
I could not pray
God help me
That was the last room
And now I walk shackled towards the light
And by God, have I waited for this blessed
      moment
And by God, have I waited, because no death
      can be worse
Than what I have suffered, and would suffer
      more
If they did not kill me now
These men, I cannot hate them
I do not have the strength
They believe they are good because
They are doing this in God's name
According to God's will
They are doing this for their God
And before I die although I will cry God is
      Great
When they say there is only one god
And his name is Allah
I wish I would have the courage to tell them
That is a lie, there is more than one God by
      that name
Because their God is not my God
Their God is a cruel, brutal, stupid God
Who makes them cruel, brutal, stupid people
And mine is not like that
But of course I will not tell them
Because they would take me back in

And do more terrible things to my body
And by my God, I do not have that degree
Of courage for my convictions
So I go now up these steps
To hear the cheering of the crowds
And feel the soft green turf beneath my feet
And fill my mind with those thoughts
To numb the cut of cold steel at my throat

Santa Eulària, Eivissa, October 2017

Trophy

A hunter always brings back a trophy
A river stone, wild herbs,
Or ivy-clinging icicles.

Terre Rouge, Alès, France, December 2010

Properly speaking this is not my poem but Mohammad Kabir's, from Kabul. In 2014 he was said to be 105 years old, and these are mostly his words, as reported in the press. I have rearranged them a little (but surely not as artfully as he arranges the flowers in his garden), and added only a very little, let us say, as glue, but in keeping with Mohammad's own account...

The Gardener of Kabul

I am an old man now
All my life I have lived in the shadow
Of the palace of Darul Aman

As a child I played in its gardens
With the children of the king
Patiently I tended them

Through years of peace and years of war
Until the jihadis came
And ruined everything

I had to leave my garden
But since five years I am back
Growing food for the soldier boys

Oh, it was so different then
Green lawns, fruit trees all around
Family picnics, and the sound

Of music, they would stay all night
With the summer moon above
And everything you saw was from paradise

So again I made the garden bloom
With seeds I brought from home
Which the soldiers helped me plant

Look, I am an old man now
But if I look younger than my years
It is because of this green garden

I am a poor man too
And can go without good food
But I cannot live without seeing green leaves

And beautiful flowers
Every flower is a symbol of paradise
And I am in paradise when I am here

One of the soldiers said
Green is happiness, green is peace
Who does not like that?

Santa Eulària, Eivissa, October 2017

If I am in doubt about how to behave in any situation in life, I go back to first principles, above all, integrity. There may come times in life when this is put to the test...

Why I Do Not Lie for You

My friend, you are special

In your suffering, you are special
In your sadness, you are special
In your fright, you are special
In your tears, you are special
In your sacrifice, you are special
In your strength, you are special
In your combativeness, you are special
In your concern, you are special
In your kindness, you are special
In your generosity, you are special
In your forgiveness, you are special
In your love, you are special
In your friendship, you are special

But all this becomes ordinary
And poor
My friend, if I lie for you

My suffering for you, becomes poor
My sadness for you, becomes poor
My fright for you, becomes poor
My tears for you, become poor
My sacrifice for you, becomes poor

My strength for you, becomes poor
My combativeness for you, becomes poor
My concern for you, becomes poor
My kindness to you, becomes poor
My generosity to you, becomes poor
My forgiveness of you, becomes poor
My love for you, becomes poor
My friendship for you, becomes poor

All of it becomes ordinary and poor
Do you understand why, my friend
I do not lie for you?

Santa Eulària, Eivissa, October 2017

If one walks about the coastline of my home island, one comes across many pretty little secret bays that can only be accessed on foot or by boat. Far from the beaten track, they have no beach concessions to clean them up, and very sadly, they are invariably strewn with mountains of plastic, most of which is water bottles. One thinks, if there is that much on one tiny beach, how much is floating around in the sea? And all of it was put there by human beings...

Out of Sight

Out of sight and out of mind
Is a saying for the blind
Who'll never cast a look
About this pretty little nook
You throw a bottle in the sea
In Barcelona, Beirut, Benghazi
And though it seems out of the way
It turns up here in this bay
Chuck it in the river, far away,
In Manchester or Mandalay
Though it's far and out of reach
It ends up here on this beach
This world's a mystery and it's magic
But when we wade through tides of plastic
The magic's black, and we, my friends,
Are tragic

Sant Miquel, Eivissa, October 2017

Human beings have accumulated all sorts of crutches - practical and cultural ones - which give us the (false) impression that we understand what's going on, that we are in control, and to keep us from dying of fright. Why not try to do without them for a few hours or a day, and face the naked truth? We may find it uplifting to our spirit...

No Signposts Now

No timepiece to mark my day
No signpost to show my way
No contour lines across a map
To tell me where the land is flat
Or how steep will be the hill
And no degrees to mark the chill
Nor weather men to let me know
How and where the wind will blow

No messages on the phone
To keep from being alone
Or tell me I exist
An item on your list
No labels to attach
No expectations to match
No identities to confuse
No masks to bemuse
No flags to proudly wave
No gains for me to crave
No scapegoats to blame
No image to maintain
No story to be spun
No prizes to be won

No claims to defend
No statements to amend
No proofs to make me see what's true
No fences around my world view
No lines drawn in the sand
No theories to misunderstand
No ologies to deceive
No isms to believe
No recondite abstractions
Esoteric speculations
No quantum fields, no big bang
No chakras, pneuma, yin or yang
No ego, superego, id
No guru, super-dogma, creed

No rocky cairns, no coloured stones
No crystal balls, no piles of bones
No mystery symbols to revere
No formula to lead from here
No reason and no rhyme
Not here, not now, not this time
Not for what I want to know
Not to where I want to go

Right now

What is real
Is a presence and a feel
Of sun, of wind, of clouds
The moon and stars around
The mountains, hills and vales

Deep gulleys and broad dales
Peaks stark on the skyline
The ins and outs of the shoreline
The rattle of the tumbling stream
The morning valley's rising steam
The vital tremble of the trees
The changing hue of the seas
The smell of soil and rock and brine
The scents of rosemary and thyme
A falling rock, a running hare
Immensity all and everywhere
This and the earth beneath my feet
Are all I know and all I need
To guide me from here to there
For wherever they will lead
Is where I know
I want to go
Right now

Sant Miquel, Eivissa, November 2017

Ah, love! The greatest motivator. Here's a love poem medley (for Clouds Woman)...

Four Love Poems

The Light in Her Eyes

As she looks at me across the table
A peculiar light which is part the candle's
      reflection
Part the moistness of her eye
And part mystery too
Makes her eyes smile from inside
Or, standing embraced
When she holds my face with her gaze
Serene, confident, languid, unrestrained
If I were to describe the light in her eyes
I should need the language of heaven

Santa Eulària, Eivissa, 2001

Morning Snow

Morning snow
She, at the window
Watching it alight
Soft as love
A pearly sky
She, looking high
Says it's so white

Like feathers
Of a dove

Conegliano Veneto, Italy, 2005

Borneo Skies

Watching her sleeping
Night cries for her beauty
Dawn's dew is made of his tears
Day awakens to her gentle breathing
With a kiss takes the sleep from her eyes
But I'll stay just a little while longer
She sighs
Turns over, and dreams
Of Borneo skies

Santa Eulària, Eivissa, August 2017[8]

She Gave Me This Afternoon

Day's heat calls a breeze
Rustling leaves on pepper trees
Like her fingers through my hair
To wipe away my every care
Cicadas scream under the sun -
A second, a day, a year are one

---

8   The first three lines of *Borneo Skies* were first published as a standalone
poem in *Three Line Poetry Issue 46*, Prolific Press Inc., 2017.

While under head her heart, her breast
Breathe their rhythm without rest
Her scent is earth in poppy bloom
Opium in the afternoon
She fills my nose, my brain, my eyes
As I fly in brilliant cobalt skies
Then sweet sleep, deep, in purple mist
Lovers' souls the spirit kissed
She gave me a poppy bloom
She gave me this afternoon

Santa Eulària, Eivissa, August 2017

Have You a Day?

Have you a day?
Then run like the salmon!
Rise like the mayfly!

Terre Rouge, Alès, France, December 2010

About the Author

"While still on the road, learner, hunter of icicles, drinker of
Khayyam's wine, some kind of healer."

Originally from Essex, Robert grew up in the south of England
before seeking his fortune in foreign lands, first in Italy, then in
Spain. His home now is on the beautiful Mediterranean island of
Ibiza with his beloved Clouds Woman, who keeps him grounded
and disabuses him of any notion that he might be in any way
perfect. He makes himself useful and earns a crust by providing
health care to the local community. He loves to spend time walking
the woods, cliffs and coastlines of his island home, and torturing
some apology for music out of his mandolin. He loves solitude,
bodies of water, forests, observing the beauty and the harshness of
nature, and (quixotically) pondering the imponderable mysteries of
life. He has two grown up children of whom he is extremely proud.
This is Robert's first book of verse. His poetry is inspired by the
beauty and mystery of the world around us, the natural
environment, the human condition, and the greatest motivator of
them all, love. Robert's other works include a guide to managing
stress and a technical book on acupuncture.